2015

LAS GRÚAS

CRANES

Dan Osier

Traducción al español: Eida de la Vega

PowerKiDS
press.

New York

For Tristan Yip

Published in 2014 by The Rosen Publishing Group, Inc.
29 East 21st Street, New York, NY 10010

Copyright © 2014 by The Rosen Publishing Group, Inc.

First Edition

Editor: Amelie von Zumbusch
Book Design: Andrew Povolny
Photo Research: Katie Stryker

Traducción al español: Eida de la Vega

Photo Credits: Cover, pp. 11, 17, 19 iStockphoto/Thinkstock; pp. 5, 9 AlexKZ/Shutterstock.com; p. 7 LittleStocker/Shutterstock.com; p. 13 Apostrophe Productions/Workbook Stock/Getty Images; p. 15 Artit Thongchuea/Shutterstock.com; pp. 21, 23 Dmitry Kalinovsky/Shutterstock.com.

Library of Congress Cataloging-in-Publication Data

Osier, Dan.
 Cranes = Las grúas / Dan Osier ; translated by Eida de la Vega. — First edition.
    pages cm. — (Construction site = En construcción)
 English and Spanish.
 Includes index.
 ISBN 978-1-4777-3298-4 (library)
 1. Cranes, derricks, etc.—Juvenile literature. I. Vega, Eida de la. II. Osier, Dan. Cranes. III. Osier, Dan. Cranes. Spanish.
IV. Title. V. Title: Grúas.
 TJ1363.O8518 2014
 621.8'73—dc23
                        2013023109

Websites: Due to the changing nature of Internet links, PowerKids Press has developed an online list of websites related to the subject of this book. This site is updated regularly. Please use this link to access the list:
www.powerkidslinks.com/cs/cranes
Manufactured in the United States of America

CPSIA Compliance Information: Batch #W14PK3 For Further Information contact Rosen Publishing, New York, New York at 1-800-237-9932

Contenido

Contents

¡Las grúas son enormes!
Levantan cargas muy alto.

Cranes are tall! They lift loads
up high.

Las puedes ver en
sitios de trabajo.

You often see them on
job sites.

La parte larga de la grúa es el brazo o pluma.

The long part of a crane is the boom.

9

Algunas grúas tienen **estabilizadores** para evitar volcarse.

Some cranes have **outriggers**. These help them not tip over.

11

El **operador** se sienta
en la cabina.

The **operator** sits in the cab.

13

Los soportes giratorios
están debajo de la cabina.
Permiten que la cabina gire.

The rotex gear is under
the cab. It lets the cab
spin around.

El **encargado de maniobra** le dice al operador adonde ir.

The **signalman** tells the operator where to go.

Hay grúas móviles que tienen orugas en lugar de ruedas.

Crawler cranes have tracks instead of wheels.

Las grúas torre son muy altas y se fijan al suelo con concreto.

Tower cranes are very tall. They are set in concrete.

¿Te gustan las grúas?

Do you like cranes?

23

PALABRAS QUE DEBES SABER / WORDS TO KNOW

(el) operador

operator

(el) estabilizador

outrigger

(el) encargado de maniobras

signalman